Now I Understand

Marius Burokas

About the translator

Rimas Uzgiris is a poet, translator, editor and critic. His work has appeared in *Barrow Street, AGNI, Atlanta Review, Iowa Review, Quiddity, Hudson Review, Vilnius Review* and other journals, and he is translation editor and primary translator of *How the Earth Carries Us: New Lithuanian Poets.* Uzgiris holds a Ph.D. in philosophy from the University of Wisconsin-Madison, and an MFA in creative writing from Rutgers-Newark University. Recipient of a Fulbright Scholar Grant, a National Endowment for the Arts Literature Translation Fellowship, and the Poetry Spring 2016 Award for translations of Lithuanian poetry into other languages, he teaches translation at Vilnius University.

Now I Understand

Marius Burokas

Translated from Lithuanian by Rimas Uzgiris

The translation of this book was supported by the
Lithuanian Culture Institute

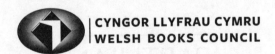

Parthian, Cardigan SA43 1ED
www.parthianbooks.com
First published in 2018
© Marius Burokas 2018
© Translation Rimas Uzgiris 2018
ISBN 9781912109449
Design and layout by Alison Evans
Printed by Pulsio

Contents

Part Four: New Poems

Because we construe
something important from trees and locomotives,
smell weeds on a hot July afternoon and feel
augmented.

– Jack Gilbert

Launderette

So many girls with highlighted hair
folding their underwear
to the drone of washing machines
neon
and the TV news

Stealthily, I watch
them perform the ritual
baskets full of underwear
with the lingering scent of flesh

So serious
so pretty
and so focused these girls
who don't know me at all
bending over their brimming baskets

A foreign language
foreign bodies
and foreign me
quickly stuffing
his rags
into the washing machine's throat

His chest tightening
alone
and completely naked
the Lithuanian poet

Part One

from *Ideograms* (1999)

I step out of my dream through
gates of bone: the butcher's shop
Theseus holding a cubit of pure
green baize, Hieronymus sounding
like ranunculus, a girl
rolling a hoop – all fitting
into the sun-scorched street
between the gates of bone and waking

Completely accidentally,
I stumbled into hagiography, a paperback
with purple letters on golden ground,
a prestigious publisher, the photograph –
black and white? As if mugged by heretics,
only the author's suffering is coloured
as in that film about the man who saved Jews.
I used to lay scattered through
various cities,
for example, my toes
were fitted out expensively
in a spacious flat full of mirrors
and film cameras,
where people would come and go,
behaving so indecently
that even St. Anthony would blush.
I preferred resting in cathedrals or out of the way churches,
kissed to the point of shining in cool
shadowed darkness, empty of thought, until
one morning, completely accidentally
my scattered bones shivered with joy
upon hearing the trumpet sound,
and I rose from the dead, feeling the snap
of sound connection – body and soul.
The very best publishers
were competing for me,
classics like Penguin, Gallimard,
HarperCollins,
until this one freckled knave
in a plaid jacket, with only one nostril,
talked me into this here
book out of which I gaze at you,
thinking—

My shelves are full of Prospero's books.
Their pages go bald every night
and the servant sweeps letters off the floor
in the morning. My memory
has weakened, and I can't place
the face in the mirror whenever I laugh or cry.
I've forgotten how doors squeak when they open,
how fats sizzle, and how the jasmine bush smells at dawn.
Every night, the ceiling rises up to the sky,
and the floor sinks down into hell.
Every night, I dream of saints
dressed up in shiny clothes,
sobbing with their backs turned to me.
Astrological signs have no meaning.
My hands have broken out in spots, and the mechanical
Turk with whom I played chess has broken down...
I'll probably have to move to a different island,
squeezing two obols into the hands of the boatman.

I wake as if suddenly pushed out of the womb,
raised by the piercing assault of sirens on the air,
I rip myself from the chair, like a malleable
lump of damp clothes, still dusted by dreams,
and I run – cutting my hands, feet, chest
on shards of glass,
I recall the secret art of embalming,
primitive religious rituals,
and a dull stone paring knife
whose memories of skin still ache—
I run – having left behind a sagging mattress,
a blinding white bed, whose sheets now dance in flames,
my heartbeats deafen me,
yellow canaries thrashing in a cage,
I run through reddish grain fields,
a sky like mother-of-pearl
gently pierced and strung, puckering like lips,
pure, limpid
dew falls over my body—
I run – until, in the middle of a grain field,
by an old maple, on a spot between the stones
of former farms, they suddenly shoot me,
and stand around, drinking by turns from a bottle,
the damp, black leather of their shoes shining,
while dogs breathe clouds of steam
that spread through the sky—

the snapshot taken by my retinas will show
only the gigantic eye of the sky,
looking at me, looking
at all of you

no one saw death's rider—
only in the already purple vineyards,
only in the hollowed-out amalgam smile,
only between clogs and the twining hands
of the apple tree, within pleats of clothes
and between the lion and the hermit
can you see the quiet autumn come—
the steed's hooves are wrapped in golden
thongs of straw

Part Two

from *Conditions* (2005)

Apologia for My Self

i'm an arrow in Sebastian's blood
a pencil of bone
that has slipped from my fingers
in a berserk fit of writing

i have defined myself
determined my place and rank
to stand until
i fall into obscurity

i'm a silver pipe
stuck in the word's throat
air escaping like a whistle
through my opening

i have disappeared from portraits
been drunk in still-lifes
and will not die from modesty

i have already heard
of myself

After Work Blues

alone after work
a beer and a thriller
on a motley planet
where I kneel down
and create this picture
for myself:

– through the glass, July weather
cools in twilight, children's shouts
       hang in the air
and a neighbour leads out
her shambling Rottweiler

and you
my legend, my myth,
close your eyes
and say:

– open me sleeping
with loving hands
       doorman
       box-mover
do not distinguish, there in the dark,
       you from me

only leave in the morning
through blinds drenched in sun,
loving and strong
– – – – – – – –

but—
you fumble your way
to bed
and the planet grows pale

Interior I

A revolver sits in sauce. A blond head
hangs out of a picture frame. A plant
in the corner loses leaves. Everything gone
yellow, art deco, rotting. Needles of sun
poke through honeyed curtains. A table
stacked with books, an Arab teapot, tea-roses,
hills gone blue with cold. Emptiness.
Only a sad dog on the bookshelf
bobs his head like a good Confucian.

Interior II
For A.

Ledges. Clothes. Shed here in the morning,
shed there in the evening. Water in the bath,
water cut with wine. A hair where you would never
expect to find one. Guilty sheets. Rings
of sleeplessness spot the furniture.
A cryptography of branches in the window.
Everything divided by two. In half-shut doors—
the sneering tongues of hinges.

Conditions

Again, I come face to face with violence.
You find yourself dialing the number—
pressed into black vulcanite, breathed into.
Yes, I felt remorse, because I killed.
Yes, I felt remorse, because I ate and wrote.
I am too ashamed to help anyone.
All it takes is a whistle to close me up.
To cover me over.
You will get no satisfaction from this.

So I unravel myself from my body,
plastering up a sticky cocoon.
I grow strong for autumn, for blackness.
I clutch at a tree trunk.
But this is just a game.
A game. Because nothing hurts.

Nor any pathos for you—
just laughter, and the stained glass
of wings on a sunny morning.

Interior IV
For Sarah

Awakened in the hush of heaving
cobwebs. Sunlight, plastered
with wet leaves, caresses concrete.
'Your place is like a trapper's hut,'
she says, 'all wooden floors and shadow.'
Coffee keeps me quiet. On her side—
sand cuts salt and clouds. On mine—
cats melt into trees. Later, the aeroplane
divides us.

Cave-dwellers

All those people, still seated
in their cars, in the afternoon
before it ends, work already done.
One hour, two, three.
They wipe their sweaty hands
on trousers, or on the seat.
They smoke, and gaze into nowhere.
A feeling of being digested, slowly,
inside intestines, inside the intestines of others,
inside a Japanese, a Russian box,
inside the box of God:
packed together in layers, decorated
on the outside with satellites.
And further, further, all is unclear to the eye.
One hour, two.
In no hurry, they ignite their engines
and turn out of forgotten streets.

With Maria Kodama, 1976–1977

For J. L. B.

typographical swarms, my face
brushing the paper, walking,
feeling our city, with a cane, *señora*,
my spiral hieroglyphs, my jaguar
released so long ago,
the notarised clouds and sky,
my neat Swedenborgian hair, *señora*,
my horse's face, long fingers,
my slowly changing eyes

what is it?

– I'm going blind,
slipping as if into water,
sinking

– I perceive,
grasping the plum-like flesh of your hand,
señora, a piece of paper brushing my face, and behind my back—
the rustling of books

Human and Oyster

I'm the ear of a snail—
do you feel
the spaces chewed out
by God, evolution and time?

But they're always filling up,
sentimentally swollen,
opening like Aphrodite—
all humidity and needles, liquid
and the polyps
that weigh boats down

Turning over into self, into being—
openings like soft gloves,
churling material
leading you,
giving itself to you, breaking
as you crack
turning into stone
and trembling
pink flesh

kats

I see you with my eyes closed
smoking nervously
like a cat on a hot tin roof
on a small balcony
mosquito bites marking lithe hands

burning up inside
while I sleep
until the streets are left with
only the cool air and trees
taxis and drunks

we don't speak
we don't make love
we live next to each other
between naked walls
and old wallpaper

nights I hide in sleep and alcohol
mornings I sneak out furtively
through the doors

fearing and hoping
that I won't find you
when I return

how we were seen
one October morning

a plump girl smothered in chocolate
her coat too tight
sitting in the back seat
staring
at you – at all of us—
wearing glasses – animalistic
in wonder
not one glass clinks
in the still sideboard of her soul
not one dog barks
in the darkness of her brain
she has just returned with her parents
chock-full
of chronic fatigue
she likes
to close herself up in her room
and cut thread
snip
snip
snip

Lithuanians 5

questionnaire

why doesn't anyone give me
what I want
for free?
why is the fence high, the host angry
and the grapes sour?
why, God,
have you turned away from us?
why does Lithuania
not stretch from sea to sea?
and where, dammit,
are the rest of our ethnic lands?
why don't I have a Visa Gold, IBM, Rolls Royce
or Klaipēda Furnishings?
why am I afraid, obeying
only the law and governmental decrees
while ignoring the catechism's truths?
why are Jews and communists
guilty of everything?
who is my neighbour really
and for whom does he work?
why don't I know
how to use a dish-washing machine?
why is someone
always following me?
why does the television set
never show anything?
where does the money go?
mouse, mouse, for whom does the blossom bloom?
where did I put my blue
jumper, black jacket
and grey trousers?

when will it all
finally end?
so?

well,
let's go to a bar
let's watch the rain
through a window
and get deathly drunk...

so,
are we going?

it's on me

Part Three

from *I've Learned How Not to Be* (2011)

stiffened sidewalk joints
bring me home

by crumbling church corners
home
by shrouded spaces
seeded with swollen lanterns
home

where in the light
we close the lid
and chimney smoke changes
languidly into whales

that swim the night's sky

home
my city, bring me
home

squint-eyed laundry, fat
women, drunk men
bring me home

name, voice recording, crumbling wall
dependence
bring me home

ravings, treachery, lies
hatred, love and kisses
touching cheeks

how beautifully
the crosses and steeples bleed

bring me home

greenish glass, dog rose shrubbery
pre-morning dew, and the first shivers
of a trolley bus wire

bring me home
my city, going home—

Sick Sick Weekend

We went quietly towards the kindergarten through slushy snow. We had to be careful – not many of us anymore – public drunks. And such an occasion! – the clear night, stars, silent peeping satellites flying by... Almost no wind. A smattering of trees. We trudged on through freezing filth, tossing our heads back from time to time. If we could just get to the hut, we thought. Shelter, straw, tranquility, vodka. A child, snoring softly, freshly born. And we in the corner there, by the poorly caulked doors, where snowflakes pile in.

✕✕✕

In the city, quarantine
and mourning, everyone
waits for snow.

on the facades, and
in the streets—
an indelible hideousness.

witches have multiplied.
they publish glitzy
books
about themselves.

shamans in the gateways
peddle amulets,
whose spells
have long gone stale.

Belarus, Poland—
burning fences
everywhere.

overturned trucks
with the contraband
of winter.

meat is sold
by the road,
virtually free.

animals have emigrated,
along with the connoisseurs
of sacred script,

and any woman
who could walk.

only men
with fishing poles
and flags,
rocks
in their bosoms—

everyone
in one square,
so that it would be easier
to take them up
into heaven
and lock them up
until they sober.

in the window
of the facing house,
in the kitchen,
a light burns.

naked death
rummages through
the refrigerator.

it's her
yellow jackboots
that shine
when she walks
the streets.

she notices me
and nods.

see you soon.

Uroboros

I'm a kangaroo. I see a fence, feel it too. The fence stings me, but it kills the yellow dogs. Everything here is hot and red. I hop, hop and hop as if wound up. If I stop – I'll die, or so it feels, the air vibrating around withered trees.

It's true: there is a way out. A teacher calls to us. His tree is green and full of fruit. His smile is like a fence without a charge – whether you jump it or not. We try. He waits. We die by the dozens. Those who make it receive the mercy of his favour: lightning out of the clear blue sky, or the rest of your life as a koala: to crawl, to eat, to die. To kill. Eucalyptus.

The teacher smiles from the other side of the fence: he calls out to us, but accepts no responsibility.

He has hired a guardian: the snake rolls around and around, and eats. And eats itself. It doesn't rest, never forgetting that it watches over us. Vanishing animals on a vanishing continent.

Oh, if only this were Europe.

The Belt

What nourishing
Nostalgia
These Frosted Flakes

Turn back the cold past
And still
It breathes on you

Like the reaper
Who, as we know,
Cuts us down
In our very bloom

Hot and
Cursing

We want to howl
In a scented field
But I go
Where I am sent

Small

Ruffled

My father
Waits for me

Holding Orion's belt
In his hands

Fog

I saw fog
flood lakes
hanging islands in the air

my lake
is flooded
my islands
hung high
as in Swift

> – you understand
> how everything tapers:
> visits
> embraces
> teeth and hair—

the fog will rise to your eyes
and you'll lose your lover's scent
even though you flew
like a moth to that flame

drinking will discolour
your tongue
as wit turns viscous
and eloquence stutters

> – still, you can always grope
> with dull fingers
>
> to close the clasps of oblivion

Jewish Cemetery, Zarasai

barberries burn
between the heels of stones
spitting snow

Being's Dotted Line

Can it be
that I remember
only heat
and nature's blank

for when I emerged
from recurring attacks

of darkness
in a kind of muck

I walked
drank
wrote

finding nothing
to hang on to

while the walls of the city
broke no bones about it

and I didn't even scrape
myself on stone
or lose so much as a finger

I learned quite well
how not to be

groping my way
to the light switch
and
to oblivion's clasp
and

under sheets of twilight
and
over wasted plains

Now, I don't stay
anywhere
for long

I never have time
to tell the story

of how dismally
we all end up

and how happily
we celebrate after

Instructions for Building an Ant-hill
for Edgaras

To begin with, you have to spit on the ground for a long time, earnestly, with clean, white spume. Next, bite and chew, bite and chew. Then toss together what you like. A refuge of crumbs, a cabin from clay, a shelter of sticks and straw. Spit-smear it like a cake. Scratch out some openings, a flue. Invite friends and relatives. Raise a ruckus for three days, four nights. Go out to the porch early in the morning, in bare feet, and look: some stare at fog, some at the clouds, some at the highway – then drive everybody out. Bring home a little mother, breed a whole brood, multiply until the get doesn't fit. Then baptise them all, raise them, marry them, drive them out of the house. Later, paste up the openings, leaving only the flue and a key around your neck, some logs, the domestic beast. When the animal croaks, lock the doors, take a bottle, go out to the porch and sway on the swing for a long time. Until it freezes.

Incantation

It had to begin
From blood
Patching itself up out of hopes
Sweet sweat and sighs

It needs to quietly tap out
Its embryonic
Little ABCs

It needs quite a lot
It's curious
And afraid

We move quietly through the furniture
And life
Afraid to scare it off
So cute and so small
So strange

I've stopped swearing

She eats everything

And we

We
By the grace of God
Are not alone

Station–Dzūkų St.

The station sounds every night. Sad beastly trains rumble by. A checkpoint on the pedestrian bridge: those in possession demand more from the meek. The moon is a gypsy knife gleaming through smog. A dive bar along the way: blue Hopper ghosts. Beer, drunken brotherhood, a haggard dog across the road. All of us here are over the edge. Farther on, there are the fumigated hills in which we have no faith. Children—whom we fear. Trees which turn to snakes below ground. At dawn – only at dawn – the station seems like snug stables. When you returned, you saw how the locals soap the sides of trains. You hear shouts, sometimes sun and wind from over there: where we will ride.

Part Four

New Poems

Home Again

Above the city, neither antennas, nor bushes
(trapped within them, the wind whines, which, evidently, is
   not ours)

the sky
open to nothing
the sun and the moon
wicks extinguished by fingers
(redemptive darkness flows between homes)

I recognise
these, my concrete innards
the rusty gums of mailboxes
vases covered in cobwebs
sideboards in the corners gone wild
(and the elevator shaft with sooty miners)

my neighbour
has taken his white horse from the balcony
(he rides it down the stairs, holding a souvenir lighter)

the hawthorns outside the window are probably mine
mountain-ash
hawthorns
mountain-ash
hawthorns
(in circles, in rows, and further – carriages and Volkswagens
roll down the street, the steppe and mountains behind)

this, my wind-strained landscape
the crooked perspective
a sore for the eye

I would enumerate further, but it is already easier, easier
(I can breathe again, it grows dark, I can't see)

you cover it with your dark palm
your calm palm

all of this horror
(this blessing)

⋇⋇⋇

powerlessness, vanity—
i repeated

> *– the city was oppressed*
> *by a stone of heat*

i cut down
those words
pulled out
syntax's cartilage
ripped out the bones
of phonemes

reality wavers
language breaks
into the throat
with ache and lightning

> *– the city was oppressed*
> *by stones of heat*

only its labyrinths
and butcher shops,
only its graves, morgues,
and churches

are cool

language unplugged
hardens

like a drop of wax
on a stone wall

Townspeople
(the other side of an old poem)

town carnivals
and songs. no one
waits for tomorrow.

drizzle. packed
streets. a jumble
at your feet.

we all depart
our dwellings
quickly. smiling
psychotics. we
buy sausages
whittled spoons
caramelised sugar
roosters.

we don't look
up. avoiding
eyes. glancing
furtively. dragging
our children behind.

who are we?
townspeople out
for the holiday. unarmed
covetous predators.
fearful and polite.

our good – in a box.
our hearts – in our mouths.

because tomorrow
(no, no, it won't come
no need to think...)

because tomorrow
they close
the gates cover
the mothers of God
take down
the stalls

because tomorrow
they separate us
into the red and
the blue.

because tomorrow
we'll grab
our loved ones
by the throat.

Pitiful
Vilnius angels

with large arses

blinding white
fright

written out
of all the heavenly
battles

banished
to our city
banished and sentenced

to solitude
and to tedium's
temptation

we know
they must be so
who shepherd us

until we suffocate
in their plumes of sleep

– how much blackness
from childhood up until now?

the knoll of
teeth

no bones
ever broken
a red ball
in the lungs—

i took such an inheritance away
from the house by the forest
a house by a slaughterhouse:

fuel oil floated down the river
sleds flared
on snowy hills

– how much blackness now?

it has faded to grey

an old bandage
like police tape
fences off the present:

i look at myself—
worked over
with fingers covered in ink

and feel nothing

The capacious lungs of wind
blow through bones and meat. Letters
are no longer mine. I won't be
scooping a handful, like tadpoles.
At least my fingers won't hurt
in the water of words. But the pool
holds no image of me. No voice.
Nothing chirrs in the heat,
nor wiggles by the roots. I don't
believe in you. No. Only the wind
wheezes. It scratches the sky
with its horns, before tipping
down, breaking firs,
ripping off roofs. It blows
through bones and meat
with the last scent
of my soul.

Vocatives

life without God is possible
life without God is impossible
> Tadeusz Różewicz, 'Without'

I

God is
dark water
that scoops me up
with my mouth full
of crustaceans
myself a shell
a cuirass
filled with God's water
grace
that washes
and subsides

it leaves me chapped
un-accepting
of what I cannot catch
unworthy
open
a shell
or empty armour
God is dark water
carrying me
relaxed

God is the dark water
of my city's stream

II

please, god,
leave all else
for later

now, just
shave me with your wind
like a fish—

with all my scales
my bristle
and my rind

let go of me
and this itchy, hiccupping heart

on the sticky highway
of death

just turn away

III

1.
o god,
what offending creatures
steam in me

cooked by concern

2.
...
i don't read
your scriptures

afraid
of a greater light

3.
...
the white lightning
of a birch
rends
a bent back
from nonbeing

this is what
i always
prayed for – humility

4.
...
how i rummage
in memory
searching for signs

but darkness
places there
a radiant
dot

White Death

with bony feet
she rattles the flagstones
at five in the morning
just like the poets said

she passed me by in childhood
as I lay in a glass box
having screamed out
the choking, warm
meat-scrap of my soul

I expected nothing
didn't get
anything

but solitude
like boiled
government-issued sheets
white
as death
stretched over
covering me

such is the legend
that's how I arrived
so I thought

I'll die this way
a toad
will crawl up
onto my swollen
heart

and squeeze

white death
with bony feet
rattles

past the linden tree
past the stone wall
past summer

in Vilnius.

February

Winter's dog
licks my hand. Snow
and stones. Heads
of children glow
in windows. Pipes
have burst, a tree
has split, steam billows
as pearly light
touches glass. All states—
uncertain. Time is
a wind from the sea
that beats, blows, burns.
I needed this salt,
your skin, my chapped lips
warmed beneath your palm—

a clean life.

＊＊＊

what cannot be coughed up
from my tarry lungs
in this brightly burgeoning
month of August?

the cooling world
withdraws
and seams, joints, cheek-bones
become clear

light
becomes parchment
syrup and subsides

in the evening
there is too little of you

as we sit down together
and watch
the fog slip
from the trenches of hills

silent
like your breath
and our warmth

or like fingers
searching for other fingers

All Day

dew falls out
fog crawls in
wind climbs up

earthly elements
rage
at their chains

only we

slap
our stomachs together
like fish

Annotated Photographs

1.

Photographs – Writers

I tried to grasp you
I stared at your faces
but was never really looking
for the secrets they contain—
I was searching for mine:
whether something connects us
a thread, a cord, a tie
whether we are touched
by the same finger
whether we picked up
the black receiver in time
whether the spark pierced us
the light
when you know
it is given to you
the curtain parts
deservedly
certainly, it is deserved
those snares
that knowing
the dependence
and sweet impatience
it is deserved
reflected in every face
that same derangement
wonder
the coy audacity

haughtiness

2.

Fred Herzog, *Man with Bandage*, 1968

he cut himself shaving
and painstakingly pasted
with fingers trembling in fury
a bandaid cross on his chin
then fled as he was
in his white t-shirt

the city is empty
only widows in black
warm themselves in morning sun
while taxi drivers nap
the black widows
trace his passage
and their lips mumble

      sonny
      we heard you last night
      your dreams are dreary
      cratered
      we listened
      to your lungs
      wheeze
      and your heart pound
      we know
      you have life
      as far as your hands reach
      and death
      from head to toe

he stands
stock still

in the bracing air

three streets stretch
before him

and

the yellow light

flashing

flashing

3.

Masahisa Fukase, *The Solitude of Ravens*, 1975/1976

raven moon
raven solitude

splashes of darkness
in the trees

torn
by the raven's claw
the moon's talon

bitterly
you caw
raven

now break
the bank's ice

raven

peck out
my darkness

mark
my fall
on ghostly snow

with your feet

4.

Algimantas Kunčius, *Palm Sunday by The Gates of Dawn*, 1968

outgrown coats
scratched-up boots

back bones
like cobblestoned streets

with stinging water
in their eyes
and three tongues
in their mouths

they clutch their willow fronds

- - - - - - - - - - - -

all those years
all those years
have passed

and only the crests in copper coins
have changed

5.

Jan Bułhak, *Evening Prayer*, 1900

to kneel on
the back pew
in aching cold

is there space for me?

alone
under the vault

in you, behind you
under your shell

is there?

- - - - - - - -

maybe I don't need
to ask questions

you already answered
with my life

a sleepy town on the edge
of a horror film by
some monument
a happy child drives
a dove to us nothing
will happen here
every evening
the sunset burns
out the retina and
memory so it's good
that i know i don't
want anything but
to slink through the reeds
in the gloaming by
the river to see
if the stream washed
up a cradle

U & J

bumpy backs
dainty mermaid bones

they breathe
like birds
caught in my hands

on both sides
little puffs of breath
they lie awake

and whisper
tell us a story
about the world
about jellyfish
tell us
what electricity is
how trees grow
and why
paper is white

I lie awake
hearing my
deep breaths

the most trustworthy
source of information
the philosopher's stone
an old
encyclopedia

the father
who ruined so much paper
covering
the pit of the past
with the flesh of the future

I speak
to their blank
slates

hoping

I'm right

Visby

the blood has been covered in snow
strewn with salt, with sand
then covered in snow again

hundreds of years ago

now only the fish-bones of churches
rattle the grey sky

axes no longer split skulls
everyone retains ten fingers
everyone's teeth are sound
curtains are pleated
and desk lamps comfortably
dissipate darkness

– the country is conquered
  by prosperity

– the island is flooded
  by peace

– the town is covered
  in plenty

After November 13

Our dogs have learned
not to bark

sirens howl instead
east and west

glass breaks
then blood is covered
in flowers

all is calm

at night
with open eyes
we lie beside
our cherished ones

listening
to the high
unyielding

drone of strings

✕✕✕

you are
a night-flower

a matte lily lamp

dim consolation
with milky hair

and whispers
through doors
in tenebrous light

there will never be
enough of you

grey drizzle
over spruce

dumb pain
on the stump
of my tongue
forgotten

kneeling
after sunset
in the ghostly light
of computer screens

By Holy Lake
for Ugne

i wait
until the small bright head
emerges from the water
eyes shut
frowning
red-faced
as if born again
tearing her way to the surface
again – with all her strength
thirsting to drink
of this world

this light

ineffable

only now do i understand

how much i hate
that greyness
how my ordinary life
is sticky and sweet
how order is my desire
and how this horrifies me
how peace possesses me
and loneliness drives me from home
how the trunks of pines by my house
radiate heat, how
finely the sand flows, how
green the lily's lament

now i understand

Books are my
paths
and garden

my shelter
and clinic

clutching their sentences
I gaze at the greenery
on the other side

      – the bars of your lines
        are dense

I husk
the pills of poems

smooth
like stones
by the Black Sea

but no—
I also want

I crave to be
one of those

riding
in armoured hexameter
harnessed to a chariot

gripping the reins
and a spear

shouting

flying like mad

into the stony backs
of the gods

Easy Rider

i will ride
the blazing bus in the dark
through the station
of insomniac bums
past the Soviet suburbs
of trenches, embrasures
and pill-boxes

i will ride
quietly smouldering in
an aquarium of flame
past tenement rows
through the dregs of darkness
eyeballs and teeth
shining white

i will watch
how the city closes up
into the fist of a flower
how its sandy
underground roots
stir and seek

i will ride
the blazing bus

farther
deeper

into the horrible
hospitality of nature
a damp refuge
of purling moss

i will ride
to try on wet
cold clothing

to lie
face-up
in an echoing spire

to burn out

Acknowledgements

The publisher would like to acknowledge the publications in which these translations have previously appeared:

Asymptote, The Bitter Oleander, Druskininkai Poetry Fall Anthology, Gobshite Quarterly, Hayden's Ferry Review, How the Earth Carries Us: New Lithuanian Poets, InTranslation (The Brooklyn Rail), Lituanus, Lumina, New Baltic Poetry Anthology, Spork Press.